To the best
DOG WALKER
in the World!

FROM:

better notes

© Better Notes · Kochhannstr. 30 · 10249 Berlin · info@betternotes.de · www.betternotes.de
Author and cover design: ilyamalyanov.com

Printed in Dunstable, United Kingdom

72792172R00070